Lobstah Tales

A History of the
Moby Dick/Back Eddy Restaurant
in Westport, Massachusetts

John B. "Red" Cummings Jr.

Hillside Media

Westport, Massachusetts

Hillside Media
Westport, Massachusetts

All inquires should be sent to:
John B. Cummings Jr.
Hillside Media
46 Hillside Road
Westport, MA 02790
Tel: 508.636.2831
Fax: 508.636.6831
or John@hillsidemedia.net

ISBN-13: 978-1530479061

Lobstah Tales

A History of the
Moby Dick/Back Eddy Restaurant
in Westport, Massachusetts

John B. "Red" Cummings Jr.

Lobstah Tales

Dedication

This book is dedicated to all the owners and employees of the Moby Dick and Back Eddy Restaurant since its founding in 1953.

Despite the changes, physical and emotional as well as types of food they all toiled in the vineyard with utmost dedication to fine service and quality of food.

The building appearance may have changed over the years and the type of foods have varied but the concept of waterfront dining in Westport, Massachusetts never wavered.

Thanks to the foresight of the Judson family who were followed by their friend from South Dartmouth, Gracia "Topsy" Waters and Bob and Barrie Therrien, the quaintness of the facility remained.

Aime and Rita Lafrance and their son, Richard, continued the casual atmosphere until Nancy and Roger Tache decided the facility needed cloth napkins. But it was Peter Sharp who took it up a notch and added an atmosphere of class which has been expanded upon by Chris Schlesinger and now by Sal Liotta and Aaron deRego.

To one and all thanks for your dedication to excellence over the past half century plus. And to many more.

Table of Contents

Preface

*A*ny tale about a waterfront restaurant that relies upon either lobstahmen or fishermen or both for support must include the sad with the happy.

There were many happy times over more than the half-century that the enterprises have been in business and they are told here. There were also sad times that need to be reported as well.

The sea can be dangerous and unforgiving and it has been on a number of occasions in Westport. There are tragic endings to harrowing events locally and some with local ties. The entire maritime community mourn these events.

The most recent (December 3, 2015) tragedy occurred twelve miles off Gloucester, Massachusetts, near Thatcher Island, when the lobstah boat *Orin C* capsized in thirty-knot winds and eight-foot seas and sank, taking one of the three on board to his death. The *Orin C* was built in Virginia in 1976 and owned by Westport lobstahman Captain John Borden before he transferred ownership. It ended up with lobstahman John Williams in Gloucester. Borden had named his boat after longtime local lobstahman Orin Crapo Jr.

Crapo's father was a legend on the water and docks of Westport. He studied the weather and went out to pull his pots only in good weather, without the benefit of a compass.

Fellow sailors took his lead and followed his actions. But his son, Orin Jr., was more daring. The nine-year-old could not swim. He fell overboard and held onto the pots and ropes until he was saved by his father. Strike one.

Years later, Orin Jr. was joined by two pals and they headed out into

1

the waters of Buzzard Bay. They were on a fishing boat and the boat was put on autopilot while the guys ate in the galley below on board the *Scotty*. Problem: they hit a freighter and flipped over. All were saved but that became strike two for Orin Jr.

Strike three occurred after the lobstah boat *Atlantic Sword*, with Crapo and two buddies on board, sunk. The boat was never found and the body of one of his friends, Sandy Pierce, was found in the West River in a lobstah tank that floated in the river while crewman Jack Bell was never found. Orin Jr's body was also never found. The Moby Dick served as the search and rescue headquarters for that disaster. Borden named his boat after his late friend.

There are other nautical tragedies in this book, but primarily it is a history of ownership and events in and around the Moby Dick/Back Eddy restaurant over the years.

I hope you find it interesting and informative and continue to support the restaurant so that it will be here for another half-century for the enjoyment of all.

John "Red" Cummings
Westport, Massachusetts
March 2016

THEY THAT GO
DOWN TO THE SEA
IN SHIPS
1623 — 1923

Foreword

On the early 1960s, I worked for Sheldon & Evelyn Judson at the Moby Dick Restaurant. I swept floors, picked over clams, and, when needed, was a busboy. It was considered the best restaurant in the area and, even with the use of paper plates, was considered fine dining. Evelyn was the cook and Sheldon the PR man. They were two of the hardest working people I knew.

I have many fond memories of the Judson's and Moby Dick. Evelyn would ask me to spear eels for her for lunch. She would then cook them for the two of us because she knew I was the only one, besides her, who would eat them. So we would sit down and eat eels together.

On my first night bussing, I stepped on a butter pad and went flying with a full tray, food flying everywhere, only to look up at Sheldon staring down on me. All this fun for $2.25 an hour.

There are stories that can go on and on. Moby Dick, Back Eddy, no matter what the name—it holds fond memories for many. As a hangout for locals and a place to meet new friends it has been and always will be a well of information, stories about local characters, and many, many laughs.

It is a comfort to know the restaurant and the traditions are still very much a part of Westport and will continue through the generations.

Dick Squire
March 10, 2016

☺ In the Beginning

In the beginning, it was "Pappy" and Evelyn and their daughter, Norma, in 1952. Then there was Carol in 1954, an event that played a significant role in the history of the waterfront facility (more about that in Chapter 3).

Before "Pappy" and Evelyn passed away, they transferred ownership in 1974 to "Topsy" and her friend, Jerry, who set out to run the business. The next owners, for a short time, were Bob (an airline pilot) and his wife, Barrie. A few years later, the restaurant was sold to Aime and Rita, who was assisted in running the business by their son, Richard.

The casual atmosphere of this eating establishment was preserved until 1985 when Roger and Nancy and their silent partners determined a little sprucing up was in order. Sadly, a kitchen fire ended their reign in 1991—even as others were approaching them to purchase the operation.

Peter and his future father-in-law, Jackson, saw dollar signs and took over in 1993. Peter also had grand visions for the place but sold the land and business in 2006 to a well-known chef, Chris, from Boston.

In 2007, Sal, who runs what they call the Front Side of the house, and Aaron, who is the head chef and in charge of the kitchen, joined Chris as part owners and the current facility, as we know it today, was born. Sal and Aaron maintained ownership after Chris moved on and they own the establishment as partners to this day.

This restaurant, now more than sixty years old, is located on the inside of the "Devil's Pocketbook," in Westport, Massachusetts, near the Rhode Island state line. The illusion of an unbroken coastline from the open sea on Buzzards Bay made this harbor a haven for early smugglers and Revolutionists.

Paquachuck, as the Indians called it, was a thriving port in the 1800s. During the golden age of whaling there was a fleet of more than thirty ships anchored across the harbor. Soon after this time period, rum-running became a colorful sport on the Westport River. Many of the homes along the road in The Village, like their counterparts on Nantucket, were built with "Widow's Walks" so wives could watch the departures and arrivals of their menfolk.

Then and now, the restaurant allows its patrons to enjoy some of the charm of the area while enjoying delicious food. In the 1950s, it was a lunchtime destination spot for preteen boys from Westport Harbor. It was a regular occurrence for ten-foot skiffs, each carrying two or three people, to motor up the Westport River toward the "Point" for chowdah and fritters at the "Dick"—an integral part of the maturing process in the summer months.

Located literally on the waterfront in the harbor of the Westport River, the Back Eddy Restaurant commenced operations as the Moby Dick Wharf Restaurant and Enterprises in the early 1950s, built by Evelyn B. and Sheldon B. ("Pappy") Judson.

Westport rumor has it that a fella who owned a saw mill in Freetown offered to deconstruct the old bridge for one dollar because he had worked a deal with "Pappy" to use the wood to help rebuild the Moby Dick Restaurant.

And so it was!

"The Bridge at Westport Point Mass,"
pencil drawing by Charles H. Overly

The facility is housed on land at the terminus of Bridge Street, which starts at the Westport River and ends at Horseneck Beach, and Cherry and Webb Lane, which begins at Bridge Street and concludes to the west at Tripp's Boat Yard and the Westport Yacht Club.

The long pier to deep water was constructed by "Pappy," Deacon Earle, and Manny Costa. Made-to-order skiffs were available for rent. In the end, there was very little rest for the owners.

Pen and ink sketch by Edna Leuveunk—June 23, 1959.

"The Moby Dick's Westport Point Mass,"
pencil drawing by Charles H. Overly

☉ "Pappy" Days

The average one-pound lobster is from four to seven years in age. A lobster's rate of growth is dependent upon the water temperature—the warmer the water, the larger and faster they grow. A one-pound female lobster carries about 5,000 eggs and females weighing nine pounds can carry more than 100,000 eggs. It takes between eighteen months and two years for lobster eggs to hatch. The eggs are inside the female for nine to twelve months and then on the underside of her tail for another nine to twelve months. Despite the large number, only one percent lives to the age of one month due to bad weather, oil slicks, fresh water, and the many creatures that feed on them, like cod, tautog, rockfish, other lobsters, and man. From every 50,000 eggs, only two lobsters are expected to survive to legal catching size, and lobster size limits vary by area.

The world began to change in the 1950s. World War II had ended and television began to alter the way people lived. Elvis may have swiveled into our living rooms but it was the Russians and Sputnik that influenced families to learn math and science and travel to parts unknown. President Dwight D. Eisenhower created the Interstate Highway Act and built roadways nationwide. The result was something new—people travelling from one end of the nation to the other for pleasure. They even drove to the ocean in Westport, Massachusetts, and enjoyed a meal at the new restaurant on the river.

Sheldon "Pappy" Judson was a successful contractor in nearby New Bedford, Massachusetts, which was, at one time, the whaling capital of the world. Not only was he a contractor, he also owned a tile store and hardware store in the area. His love of the sea drew him to fishing and he purchased commercial fishing boats and lobstah boats. His year-round home was in New Bedford with his businesses but his heart was his at his summer place at Westport Point—where he was kept plenty occupied. In the early 1950s, "Pappy" purchased land on the south end of the Point Bridge and together with Deacon Earle (recently retired Harbor Master Richie Earle's brother), they rented skiffs from the deep-water pier "Pappy" had built. At the end of the pier was a buying station where locals, like Cukie Macomber, would sell their catch of lobstahs, scallops, and more to "Pappy."

Next to the skiff business was a small red building where "Pappy" and his wife, Evelyn, would enjoy warm summer days relaxing in the sun. But sitting around was not "Pappy's" idea of fun. He needed to keep active even during his retirement. The red building became a lobstah pound where lobstahs were sold after delivery from his 40-foot lobstah boat, *Moby Dick Too*, captained by John Osborne in 1962, or the *Hazel M*, which "Pappy" also owned.

The beginning of Moby Dick Enterprises was born.

"Pappy" and Evelyn and Gunda enjoy a relaxing day.

14

Osborne ran into a problem on the open seas. His competition reported him to the authorities. He only had a lobstah fishing license in Rhode Island, but not in Massachusetts. Back at that time, it was not the boat but the lobstahman who was required to hold the license. Up came the pots and gear, which Osborne constructed during the winter in "Pappy's" dining room. Everything was moved to Rhode Island waters and the catch transported back to the dock at the Moby Dick for sale.

In "Pappy's" restaurant dining room resided a fish tank, inhabited by catch made off the coast, including Charlie, a sizeable tautog who liked his belly rubbed by patrons. "Pappy's" menagerie expanded. Next came a crow, soon adopted the family and was fed cat food to keep it coming back. It spent the winters in "Pappy's" jeep. But the crow turned out to be only a short-term visitor because one day it attacked Minnie Robbins' Girl Scout hat while Minnie was wearing it as she tended to her garden. Off the crow was shipped to Herb Hadfield's wild kingdom in the woods.

After the red building became successful as a result of Horseneck Beach goers purchases, "Pappy" added a sandwich shop, a fish market, and a garage. At the far west section of the sandwich shop was an unused space large enough to create a sports-wear shop tended to by their daughter, Norma, who was just out of college. She opened the Moby Dick Shop in 1953 and followed that with a shop called Silas Brown.

The empty space in the 100-foot building in 1953 worked for everyone. Norma was engaged at the time and her future husband, a student at Dartmouth College, was reading Herman Meville's classic *Moby Dick*—and so the name was born. Norma was a true historian of the town of Westport, and was involved with multiple Community Preservation and history projects. She was recognized as Westport's Woman of the Year in 2011 and created the History Room at the Westport Library. Norma dedicated her life to discovering the town's history, according to an article which appeared in *The Harbinger Newsletter* of the Westport Historical Society in Winter 2016. The Moby Dick Enterprises were very successful until the start of business on August 31, 1954, when it was all but destroyed by Hurricane Carol.

Since the facility was a casual seafood establishment, there wasn't anything on the menu in excess of $4.05—and that was the 2.5-pound lobstah. Food was served on paper plates to avoid the need for dishwashing. A child's menu was available for those twelve and

Norma, waiting for customers at the gift shop.

under for $1.25 but the food had to be ordered by the child, not the accompanying adult. Drinks were also priced according to the times. Lobstahs were delivered to floats with the bill left at the business by the local lobstahmen.

The second year in business, "Pappy" was able to acquire a liquor license for the restaurant. A bar, under the control of Ruth Ameil, was fiercely overseen by the owners to avoid any problems. Liquor sales proved profitable and the Judsons were highly successful entrepreneurs. To-go orders were also available and made by chef David Lees, who also prepared the evening meals of chowdah and lobstah. Lees spent his days working down the road at Tripp's Boat Yard, moving craft from one location to another from 4:30 a.m. He would return home to shower and start work at the Moby Dick at 5:00 p.m. If anything more elaborate needed to be prepared, hard-working Evelyn jumped into the kitchen and took over the duties. Barbara Sanford served as waitress for the establishment and Joan Sherman watched over the finances.

While the Judson family was enjoying their newly created and successful enterprises, in late August 1954, the weather in the southern Atlantic was beginning to show signs of change.

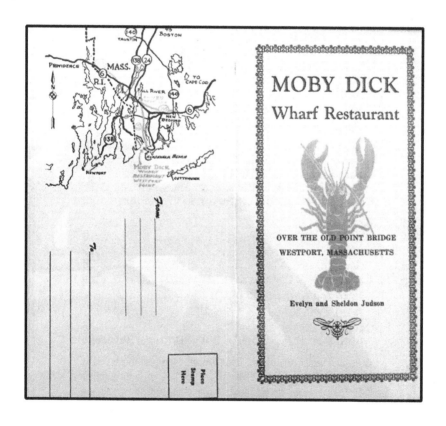

All Lobsters and Clams Cooked to Order

Cooking Time — Lobsters

Chicken (1 lb.)	20 min.
1¼ - 1½ lb.	25 min.
1¾ - 2 lb.	30 min.
Clams	20 min.

Natural sweetness and tenderness are best preserved by our own sea water steam process.

1¼ lb. Lobster	2.55
1½ lb. Lobster	2.85
1¾ lb. Lobster	3.15
2½ lb. Lobster	4.05
2 lb. Lobster	3.45
2¼ lb. Lobster	3.75
Chicken Lobster 1 lb.	2.25
Lobster Salad	3.00
Lobster Saute	3.00
Swordfish	2.25

Lobster Spread, French Fried Potatoes, Green Salad, Butter and Rolls served with above orders.

Quahog Chowder ...... large .60 small		.30
Lobster Sandwich with F. F. or Green Salad		1.60
Steam Clams with F. F. or Green Salad Roll and Melted Butter		1.75
Clams served with Lobster or Fish Dinners		1.35

Beverages

Coffee - Tea - Soda	.10
Milk	.15
Ice Tea - Coffee	.20
Ice Cream	.25

Child's Plate (under 12 years in company with grown ups)

Chopped Steak	1.25

Chips or F. F. - Salad - Roll - Butter - Beverage

Lobsters and Swordfish are brought to us daily right from the local fishing grounds.

Our Clams come from local, Cape Cod and North Shore areas then processed by us in our own tanks to produce the sweetest, cleanest clams served anywhere.

COCKTAILS
(.95)
Manhattan
Martini (Dry)
Daiquiri
Whiskey Sour
Stinger
Old Fashioned
Tom Collins

BOURBONS
(.95)
Old Grandad
Old Forester
Jack Daniels

RYE WHISKIES
(.95)
Seagram's V. O.
Canadian Club

BRANDY
(.95)
Coronet V S Q
Heublein (4 flavors)

CORDIALS
(.95)
White & Dark Creme de
  Cacao
Green & White Creme
  de Menthe
Benedictine
Drambuie
Southern Comfort

VODKA
(.95)
Smirnoff

SCOTCHES
(.95)
Haig
DeWar's White Label
Black & White
Cutty Sark

GINS
(.95)
Beefeater
Fleischman's
Gordon's

RUMS
(.95)
Bacardi
Myers

WINES
Sauterne
  (12 oz. bottle)   2.50
Pouilly Fuisse Burgundy
  (12 oz. bottle)   2.50
Liebfraumilch (crock)

BEER
Domestic
Michelob (Draft)   .60
Budweiser .... .50
Miller Hi-Life ...... .50

Imported
Lowenbrau Light   .75
Lowenbrau Dark ... .75

CHAMPAGNE
California Roma
Pol Roger
(*French imported*)

Photos and menu courtesy of Norma Judson.

③ ⓒ Heeere's Carol

A lobster can survive out of seawater for several days if the temperature and humidity are cool and moist. The lobster is native to the waters of the north Atlantic coast and is entirely different from its cousin in the Pacific.

In the early 1950s, during the infancy of television and the science of meteorology, a weather alert for rain and high winds was just that, an alert and no more. A storm, later named Carol, would pound the East Coast and particularly southern New England with 135 miles per hour wind, rain, high surf, storm surge, and flooding. Carol came to Westport with little or no warning and caught everyone along the waterways by surprise.

The storm was so strong that it ripped the Sandwich Shop off its pilings on the river and pushed it up-river before returning the building to a site across the road.

The Category 4 hurricane raced into Westport in the late morning and destroyed everything in her path, including the Moby Dick Enterprises. (The story of Hurricane Carol and its impact upon Westport can be found in another book by this author, entitled *The Last Fling.*)

"Pappy" Judson had poured all of his retirement funds, along with money raised from a bank mortgage, into this venture and for two successful summer seasons he was very profitable.

The damage to the area was so extensive that the Commonwealth of Massachusetts was forced to take "Pappy's" property by eminent domain, for a mere $17,000—a far cry from the losses he suffered. The Judson family lacked the funds to mount a lawsuit to fight the taking

THE LAST FLING
HURRICANE CAROL 1954

Fascinating Survivor Interviews - A Genuine Collectors Item

and was forced to rely on the generosity of fellow Westporter Milton E. Earle, who owned land nearby. This allowed Judson to rebuild a smaller sandwich shop and a larger store and start anew on the south side of Cherry and Webb Lane. Only the Gulf gasoline station survived on the water-side of the road and became the new Moby Dick Wharf Restaurant, where it remains today.

"Pappy" was the creative one in the family but it was Evelyn who worked the long hours in the kitchen to save money.

He spent, she saved.

They were a truely loving couple. They passed on a few months of each other. Prior to their deaths, their daughter, Norma, converted the three buildings on the south side of the street that consisted of the sandwich shop and clothing store to a store called Silas Brown that was moved up Main Road to a location that presently houses a branch of the Westport Credit Union in the Lees Market parking area. Also before the Judsons passed on, they sold the business to their friend who visited the restaurant frequently, South Dartmouth resident Gratia "Topsy" Waters, who was an heir to the Corning Glass fortune. Waters bought the restaurant in 1971 and formed the Moby Dick Wharf Restaurant Inc. and hired a friend to operate the business.

⊚ Tospy's Turn

The green you find in a cooked lobster is the liver, intestine, and pancreas. Technically, it is called tomalley. Anything red are eggs from the female, which are the size of head of a pin.

When Gratia "Topsy" Waters took over ownership in August of 1971, under the name of the Moby Dick Wharf Restaurant, Inc., she employed only seasonal help. "Topsy" paid Judson $250,000 for the business and real estate. Forty–year-old Jerry Lougganes, of Dartmouth, nicknamed "The Greek," managed the facility and his brother, Ray, worked in the kitchen, while Joan Sherman stayed on to handle the finances. Continuing as the chef was David Lees, later of the Lees Oil and Point Market fame, along with twenty-six-year-old Ruth Ameil on the bar and Barbara Sanford serving as one of the waitresses. They changed little from the highly successful and casual dining waterfront emporium that the founders had created. If anything, it became a bit more casual and perhaps a bit more profitable. Peanut shells covered the floors and beachgoers stopped by for a beverage and a shellfish treat before returning home.

It worked.

The fast-pace excitement of the restaurant business, especially at a summer establishment that was a sideline to most owners, became very intriguing. Open for business nightly, it served a limited lunch on weekends. But the bar, located on the south side (parking lot side) of the building, was open and drunk driving laws were not enforced like they are today. The bar was primarily a service bar for the waitstaff to put in orders for drinks, but a small addition allowed for seven seats for patrons to enjoy a beverage and the views. Customers would often awake the next morning not knowing how they got home. There were very few cars on Route 88 late in the night, but the safest way to get off the river area was up Drift or Main Roads.

The 1960s had been a turbulent decade for the nation. The assassination of President John F. Kennedy, the expansion of the war in Vietnam, the civil rights movement, and desegregation all caused angst that continued into the early 1970s with the Watergate scandal and the resignation of President Richard M. Nixon. At the end of the 1970s, Iran held fifty-four American hostages for 444 days until President Ronald Reagan took office, when they were released.

The bathing suit crowd jammed the spot on weekends from June through September. But it was only a seasonal summer business and was closed from October to Memorial Day. Despite the low overhead during the down months, so too was the income reduced to zero. Bank loans, taxes, and various fixed expenses (like spetic removal) still needed to be paid.

Bill Pearson, current owner of the Westport Social Club in Central Village, owned a septic removal truck that was known as "Juicy Lucy" and the truck was inscribed with the saying, "Your s—t, is our bread and butter." One day at the restaurant, using the giant straw to cleanse the system, one of Pearson's staff slipped and took a dive into the full tank.

That quickly sobered him up!

Summer revenue was required to pay winter bills. And despite her deep pockets as an heir to the Corning Glass fortune, "Topsy" saw the summer excitement turn to winter blues. Long-term prosperity was in the cards but after three years of ownership she decided it was time to sell to someone who had a passion for the business. In flew Bob and Barrie Therrien who, like "Topsy," had spent many an hour in the facility enjoying the view, food, and beverages.

⑤ ⑤ Barrie and Bob

The largest lobster ever caught was forty-four pounds. With the exception of the head and stomach, the entire lobster is edible, including the green (tomalley) and red (roe) substance in the body.

Within three years of Topsy's experiment in the business, new owners Barrie and Bob Therrien took over under the name of Moby Dick, Inc. Barrie, whose maiden name was Whittall, had been brought up in Westport on a horse farm on Horseneck Road. The married couple also owned the Sandwich Shop on the parcel to the south and the Prelude Building, with its three apartments, to the west. The apartments were eventually turned into condos and remain that way to this day. On the first floor of the Prelude, Bob ran a lobstah business and fish market. The restaurant was not an operation for a young family with three children, but they made it work.

Bob was an airline pilot for Northeast Airlines and Trans World Airlines (TWA) and then a pilot for Nabisco. While he was away, Barrie would spend the entire day at the restaurant and sandwich shop, which was open year-round for breakfast, lunch, and dinner. In addition to these duties, Barrie was responsible for transporting the day's cash receipts home (there were no credit cards back then.)

Local fishermen and lobstahmen would often take the Therrien's three young girls out in the river to catch fish and pull lobstah traps. The kids would then sell to the restaurant the small fish that they caught or clams they dug since the principal food served was either fish or shellfish.

Barrie tallying the receipts.

Most of the customers were local fishermen, except in the summer when visitors from the nearby state camp grounds on Horseneck Beach would come in for an after-dinner beverage. On one occasion, a customer, who had caught an octopus in the deep waters of Buzzards Bay, added the species to a clam basket to the delight of all the customers. The locals were all very protective of the owners.

On another occasion, a male patron, who had been over-served alcohol, became belligerent with Barrie and took a swing at her. Her children's schoolteacher was immediately evicted from the premises and rushed out by the locals. That was, however, one of the only problems they had with over-served patrons, which is remarkable for a business open all year with a liquor license.

It was during this era that the service bar was expanded and relocated to the other side of the building to encourage patrons to stay and enjoy the view. Bartender Ruth convinced the owners to install a light switch at the bar, which was used to signal incoming boats that the bar was still open if the lobstahmen arrived late at night. This often occurred when partners Paul Brayton and Richie Earle returned with their catch of lobstahs on board the *Side Show*.

No signal, bar closed!

Like during Judson's time, Bob and Barrie were adopted by local wildlife, in this case a great blue heron. If the heron appeared on the windowsill, it indicated a full moon and an interesting night to follow. It was also a sign that "Crab S—t" Manchester, a local fisherman and character, would drop in for a beverage.

The menu and the atmosphere of the restaurant remained casual, like during the days "Pappy" and then "Topsy" owned it. Bob and Barrie operated the business on a year-round basis and to make things hum in the off-season they held a variety of activities. Each Wednesday evening was movie night and periodically on Saturday night they would bring in a popular band from Northampton, Massachusetts, (The Endless Knights) who would rent hotel rooms on Rt. 6 at the Capri Motel. Holidays were always an excuse for a special event or party.

Bob Therrien relaxing at the horse farm.

On Halloween, customers would dress up for prizes and one year a patron showed up as an outhouse! First Prize!

The staff declared 1976 as the Year of the Merkin. *The Oxford Companion to the Body* dates the origin of this pubic wig to the 1450s. According to the publication, women would shave their pubic hair for personal hygiene and to combat pubic lice. They would then don a merkin. Also, prostitutes would wear a merkin to cover up signs of disease, such as syphilis. It has also been suggested that when male actors played female parts onstage, they would cover their genitals with a merkin so they could pose as women in nude scenes.

Bob Therrien in Halloween costume with his lobstah Merkin, 1976.
Photos in this chapter courtesy of Ruth Ameil.

The Oxford English Dictionary dates the first written use of the term to 1617. The word probably originated from *malkin*, a derogatory term for a lower-class young woman, or from Marykin, a pet form of the female given name Mary.

Posters were made, hats created, and a genuine anniversary party atmosphere prevailed in the restaurant led by local artist and conservationist, Herb Hadfield.

The day a patron ran through the lobstah tanks was not the result of a special event, just a harmless gesture of a man who was lucky the crustaceans did not bite his feet.

As well as happy and fun times at the Moby Dick, there were sad times. The restaurant was open all year and during the bad months lobstahmen and fishermen stayed in port. Because of this, "The Dick" was a place where everyone knew your name. Occasionally, a boat would head out into the winter roaring sea and encounter the likes of the perfect storm. On one winter day, the men of a particular boat drowned and floated back into the harbor dead. No one had survived.

Some time after the purchase, Bob, who had developed a hearing problem, and Barrie encountered some turbulence and they decided that it was time to call it quits. Cooks John Gifford and Lee Rossiter, waitresses Debby and Besty McBurney, and bartender Ruth Ameil offered to work on staff at no charge for a time if the owners would stay open. It did not. It was shuttered until the next owner purchased it at auction.

Aime and Rita Pull the Pots

You can tell a male lobster from a female by the reproductive organs and the appendages. Lobsters mate as human's do—by physical contact. Their shells are their skeletons within which they grow. As they grow, their shell splits open and is discarded with a new and larger one formed underneath. This molting occurs yearly for males and every other year for females. Through regeneration, lobsters also have the ability to grow new claws, if needed.

Aime Lafrance went off to work early one morning in the fall of 1976. When he returned home late in the day he told his wife, Rita, that he had just bought another restaurant.

Surprise!

At a mid-day auction in south Westport, the Moby Dick Restaurant, built by Sheldon and Evelyn Judson and more recently owned by Barrie and Bob Therrien, went up for sale. The Lafrances had built up the popular White's on the Watuppa in the town's north end and it was, in Aime's mind, time to expand and give their only child, Richard, a reason to become more active in the business.

This was not Aime's first rodeo. He started his hospitality business at White's Spa and then purchased the Lamplighter Restaurant and merged the two into White's on the Watuppa, as it was known, and it was flourishing as a banquet facility. In his plan, the Moby Dick would become a seasonal, casual dining facility.

They moved qualified staff from White's over to the Moby Dick: Donald Harrison became General Manager; Arthur Durand, Rita's brother-in-law, was named Chef; and three waitresses. To these folks were added three bartenders and an additional nine waitresses. Many of the waitresses were local youngsters like Pam Manchester and Carrie Trowbridge Law (Pam worked there between 1977 and 1982). As a teenager, Christopher Panos (now a federal bankruptcy judge) worked behind the line preparing the meals. Panos had worked on Dr. Dick Fitton's 47-foot wooden sword fishing boat, *Wanderer,* out of the Point. In that capacity, Panos was responsible for cleaning the catch of big fish prior to sale.

The sales often occurred at the dock of the Moby Dick Restaurant where Aime, a chain-smoker at the time, would purchase the entire fish. Panos would help prep the fish and the leftovers from the large pieces were cut up and used in one of Amie's salads. Amie never let anything go to waste. Panos eventually jumped ship to become a full-time line cook at the restaurant, because Captain Dick only fished periodically and the college student needed steady summer income. The seasonal business opened on Memorial Day and closed on Columbus Day. It was open daily for lunch and dinner from noon to 10:00 p.m. With music by the Bee Gees and "Saturday Night Fever" playing in the background, a lava lamp glowed in the corner.

It was not always sunshine at the restaurant. One morning, Arthur arrived to find that no lobstahs remained in the tanks. Between 150 and 200 lobstahs were gone. It was never divulged how they disappeared but Arthur had to replenish them for the evening meals. A call to Eddie Doan at the Westport Lobster Company on Main Road in Central Village got Arthur through the disaster until another lobstah boat arrived to resupply the busy waterfront facility.

It was not until the writing of this history that Arthur knew how the culprits got into the building. Neighborhood kids climbed onto the roof, went into the second floor office through a window—the same window used years later by Cheryl Gifford to secure her employment interview with Chris Schlesinger. The teens had surveyed the building and decided they needed to bring plastic bags to escape with their catch, which they loaded with lobstahs and took home. The lobstahs were deposited into a bathtub full of water, but many escaped by climbing over the sides and out!

Six to seven bushels of clams were tied to the docks, flushing out in the salt Westport water prior to steaming in the kitchen. Yes, one morning they too were missing. "Those damn kids," said recently retired eighty-one-year-old Arthur in a telephone interview from his

Richard, Rita, and Aime at White's in the mid 1970s.

lifelong home in Swansea. It was never disclosed who was responsible for the clam caper. It was most likely the kids but the culprits are still not known for sure. Also missing was the electric generator that was kept in front of the building.

One Saturday, a local well-known sports writer married a female athlete and they held their reception in the private room on the west side of the building. As one of the invited guests departed from the reception, the urge to put his hands into one of the lobstah tanks near the exit was just too tempting. Out came a two-pounder. Off it and he went to Rhode Island. The guest had his own stash of lobstahs in a trap but none had their claws already banded in red like this one. The thief placed the stolen booty in the lobstah pot that he shared with a friend in the waters of Rhode Island Sound. From his perch on the beach, the next day, he watched his friend motor to the pot to find the big one he has stashed there. "We hit it big time," the co-owner reported back, not noticing the banded claws. The wedding guest doubled over in laughter. Aime and Rita did not report the incident to the lobstah police.

The menu at Lafrance's Moby Dick was very similar to prior ones. Chowdah and fritters were a staple for any seafood establishment on the water. Always popular were lobstah, steamers, and a swordfish dinner with salad and corn bread. Customers selected their own dinner from the lobstah tank. Arthur served chowdah from the frozen quart containers that he made from his original recipe. After all, Arthur was accustomed to preparing and serving at White's Banquet Restaurant in North Westport, where large quantity was customary. Here, he ran a kitchen on the water with seventy-three burners for cooking lobstahs. He steamed the clams in colanders on top of these pots.

Meals were served on tables made from lobstah traps and adorned with checkered plastic tablecloths, which were easy to clean. Large sinks to wash up after enjoying a lobstah meal were placed strategically in the dining room. Adult beverages were also available from the large bar inside and pleasure craft would tie up on the dock with owners making their way to the outside service bar to refresh.

There was never any trouble at the watering hole or in the family restaurant. Fall River strongman, Joe Savitch, was a steady customer and saw to it that all the patrons respected Aime and his business. Joe kept his boat at the dock and sold freshly caught fish to the Moby Dick Wharf Restaurant for fourteen years.

Due to the proximity to the beaches, the Lafrance wharf restaurant drew upon beachgoers and state employees alike. Some of the beach lifeguards were schoolteachers with summer jobs. They were over twenty-one years old and able to go to the bar after work for a quick one before driving home. Most of the time it was a very cordial group, according to Lifeguard John Sheahan, who worked for the Commonwealth at Horseneck and at Baker's Beach down the road.

Sheahan had just departed from working the beach one day in the fall of 1961 when beach owner John Baker, 51, shot and killed Herb Straker, 55, over contested ownership of an abandoned boat that had washed up onto the beach. Baker was accused of murder but was released on bail, the only person so charged allowed.

For over nine years. Aime treated the boys well and they, in turn, looked out for the Moby Dick. Sheahan was often joined by Ray Reidy and Paul Leite, among other guards who were of legal age to drink in the over-twenty-one restaurant. Although there was no live entertainment, there was a jukebox and the lifeguards would often crank up its volume. Manager Don Harrison felt the noise disruptive to other patrons, so he evicted the lifeguards. When Aime heard the story, he directed Harrison to take a full case of Heineken beer to the boys. After all, they spent lots of money in the restaurant. On another occasion, the lifeguards had a Sunday off work and decided to go clamming. But they had no beverages and the Commonwealth's Blue Laws prohibited the purchase of liquor on Sunday. They headed to the Moby Dick dock, found Aime, and offered to buy a case from the owner. "No deal," said Aime, "but here is a case to take with you." What a guy!

On more than one occasion more than one drink would be consumed and it would get a bit rowdy in the main bar. But not for long, according to ninety-two-year-old Rita recently at her Westport East Branch riverfront home.

Apparently, in the mid 1980s, an altercation broke out among the lifeguards one afternoon. In stepped Joe Savitch and things settled down quickly. Joe was reported to have mafia ties as an enforcer, but not a made member. Joe, along with his pal Louie Alexander, who had spent ten years from 1970 forward in prison for rape, disappeared for a number of years. They were believed to have become informants for the FBI. Later, they were found dead in the Maine woods near Savitch's hunting camp.

There would be no fights in his friend Aime's casual attire facility. There was no live entertainment of any kind at any time except piped in music, recalled Rita during her interview in the summer of 2015.

Despite it being a financial success, the Lafrance Wharf Restaurant, Inc. became too much work in the summer for the family of three. It was a money-making proposition but they were tired and it was time to sell.

Enter stage left Roger and Nancy Tache, part of the loyal customer base the Lafrances had cultivated.

Grandson Sean sucking on a leg of a cull before it disappeared.
Photos in this chapter are courtesy of the Lafrance family.

7 ⊙ The Tache Take

The claws of a two-pound lobster can crush as hard as a human bite. Large lobsters can crush a heavy quahog shell with ease. They are not normally aggressive but fight defensively, or for food, or at mating time.

Roger Tache maintained a full-time position in the administration at the University of Massachusetts at Dartmouth, located about ten miles from the Westport harbor. His wife, Nancy, was a Fall River schoolteacher who had taken a leave from instructing first graders and ran the restaurant that Roger always dreamed of owning. He also saw the potential for a large real estate profit over time.

They opened the facility to the public on tax day, April 15, 1984, prior to taking on investors like Dan Bogan, who jointly owned the two parcels of land that the facility occupied. Bogan was urged to invest by a local businessman whom Bogan respected.

The building was uniquely built in the style of a fishing boat. Most likely it was designed and built by "Pappy" Judson after Hurricane Carol because he had been a contractor in New Bedford in his younger days and was a fisherman in more recent times. The first twenty feet from the entrance to mid-building was flat, but then it had a slight, gradual slope toward the river and the sunset.

The floors had what Nancy described as three-foot-square box-like covers with brass rings, which were only to be opened when terrible weather was fast approaching to allow rising river water to enter the building and be released back into the river through these holes in the floor. The current general manager and owner, Sal, explained it in more detail: "There are now twelve traps in the dining room floor to allow the rising river to relieve the pressure and stabilize the forty-eight pilings that support and stabilize the structure if and when the river rises."

Since it was a lobstah shack, there was a need for lobstahs and tanks to hold the crustaceans. The tanks held two thousand pounds of lobstahs. They were easy to come by as the port had become a haven to lobstah boats and fishermen. A lobstah boat, the *Elizabeth Ann*, owned by forty-year-old lobstahman Milton Brouilliard, delivered his catch as needed to the Moby Dick. Tragically, years later, he was washed overboard after being caught by the rope lines on a calm day and his body was never found.

The waitstaff was still talking about the USA hockey win over the Russians in the Olympics and the birth of MTV. By this time, women had flown in space and the Space Station was a beehive of activity. The

The dock and restaurant staff waiting for the lobstah boat delivery.

restaurant was flourishing. So was insider trading and junk bonds on Wall Street.

When the lobstah boats arrived at the dock they were taken to two lobstah holding tanks in the kitchen. They used two tanks—one inside the west kitchen and one alongside, available for viewing and patron selection for their meal. They were located on the main floor of the building in the ice-cold, salty water, which was filtered and refrigerated. The water came from the river below and kept the lobstahs happy until their final demise either by cooking, steaming, or broiling. The water was brought up to the kitchen by means of a series of pulleys. The lobstahs were sorted by size and placed into the proper section. Tanks were separated by the weight of the lobstahs, except for the twenty-five pounder used for entertainment value. Other large crustaceans were

fed daily with scallops, fish, or both, until a patron selected them for dinner.

The price of a one-pound lobstah had risen from the days when "Pappy" was the owner, then priced at $3.40. Back then, a gin and tonic could be consumed for eight-five cents. Prices rose as diners sat at white tableclothed tables with the charts and drawings of the town adorning the walls.

This was the era of power dinners with the likes of such well-known stars as Superman Christopher Reeves, who arrived at their dock on his sailboat with his brother, both of whom were especially tall, and actress Cloris Leachman, who came to dine one evening and ended up busing tables.

Christopher Reeves and Cloris Leachman.

The menu was fresh seafood with lobstahs brought right to the dock. Cajun dishes had become very popular during Tache's ownership, and specials like Cajun popcorn shrimp and Cajun roast beef were served on weekends were served by chefs Chris Franco and Chris Lapage in honor of Roger's chum, the famed chef from Fall River, Emeril Lagasse. Bam!

The Tache's employed fifty-four people during the summer months, Tuesdays through Sundays. They were one of the first eating establishments to offer Westport Rivers Wines and Samuel Adams beer, which were served by bartender Rob Benevides, from Fall River, in the Lobster Trap Lounge.

Franco on the dock and Lepage at work in the kitchen.

There were many suitors for the business between 1984 and the fire in 1991. A local attorney approached the owners and made an offer. A well known real estate agent also made it known that he too had a customer. But it was the inferno on the night of July 12, 1991, that closed the doors for nearly two years. Prior to this event, the building had experienced a water problem on a Sunday morning. A supply tank in the basement had let go, which moved Roger into action. He drove down the road to Baker's Beach, found John Sheahan, who returned to stop the flow of water from the tank. It saved the Taches from having to close and lose the weekend crowd and income. Sheahan was rewarded with free tickets and parking to Red Sox games for years after that!

The phone call came early in the morning on Monday, July12, 1991, from Westport Fire Chief, Bill Tripp. Nancy and Roger had barely fallen asleep when they were abruptly awakened with the news and quickly drove from their home in Fall River to the burning restaurant at the end of Route 88 in Westport.

The fire began at 1:45 a.m. in the kitchen and the blaze took over the building in a flash. According to reports, an electrical cord had been spliced and a different gauge wire had been used. A kitchen towel had caught fire. And the rest is history. If it was not for the outstanding effort of firefighters—mostly all volunteer at the time, the restaurant may have burned to the ground, as the owners stood watching, helpless and teary-eyed. A few days later, the Taches announced that they planned to rebuild and reemploy the staff. But it was not to be. By the time a settlement was reached with the insurance company, the business was transferred to another new owner for $330,000, which was far from the offer of 1.2 million dollars that had been made to them only months before by the same person.

MOBY DICK **WHARF RESTAURANT**
ON THE WATERFRONT

Please notify your wait person
regarding any food allergies.

FROM THE BAR . . .

MARTINI	____	FROZEN MARGARITAS	____
MANHATTAN	____	BLOODY MARY	____
FRUIT DAIQUIRIS	____	COLADAS	____
(Strawberry and Peach)		(Pina, Strawberry, Melon)	

BEER

Draught		**Imported**	
BUDWEISER	____	MOLSON GOLDEN,	____
MICHELOB LITE	____	Canada	
HARPOON	____	HEINEKEN,	____
		Holland	
Domestic		BECK'S LIGHT,	____
COORS LIGHT	____	Germany	
MICHELOB	____	GUINESS STOUT,	____
MILLER LIGHT	____	Ireland	
ROLLING ROCK	____	CORONA,	____
O'DOUL'S	____	Mexico	

NON ALCOHOLIC BEVERAGES

SODA	____	JUICE	____
Pepsi, diet pepsi, teem, ginger ale, tonic.		Orange, grapefruit, cranberry, pineapple and tomato.	
MINERAL WATER	____	COLADAS	____
VIRGIN MARY	____	LIME RICKEY	____
MARGARITAS	____	DAIQUTRIS	____

APPETIZERS

ON THE HALF SHELL
Priced Per Piece

LITTLE NECKS _____   OYSTERS _____
JUMBO SHRIMP _____

STEAMERS   ½ Qt. _____   1 Qt. _____
Clean'n sweet, served with drawn butter.

MUSSELS _____
Steamed in white wine, garlic and chopped tomato.

CLAMS CASINO _____
Broiled with casino butter, topped with bacon.

CLAM CAKES "AHABS'S FAMOUS"
½ Doz. _____   1 Doz. _____

HALF LOBSTER, Chilled _____
Served with tangy mustard sauce.

COLD SEAFOOD VARIETY PLATE _____
Two poached shrimp, scallops, lobster salad with aioli mayonnaise.

GRILLED SHRIMP SKEWER _____
With andouille sausage, peppers, and creole mustard sauce.

CAJUN POPCORN _____
Baby shrimp coated with crispy crumbs and cajun spices served with
our own cajun sauce.

ENTREES

FILET MIGNON _____
Choice filet of beef, grilled and served with peppered cream sauce.

GRILLED CHICKEN A L'ORANGE _____
Boneless breast of chicken grilled with an orange glaze.

BARBECUED PORK CHOP _____
Pork loin chop grilled, served with spicy BBQ sauce, and cole slaw.

WHARF MIXED GRILL _____
Shrimp, sausage, chicken and beef tenderloin grilled, served with
roast garlic and red pepper mayonnaise.

SHRIMP DIANE _____
Sautee of shrimp, mushrooms, cajun spices, served on a bed of rice.

PRIME RIB (Cajun Style) _____
Prime beef, tender and juicy.

ALL DINNERS INCLUDE YOUR CHOICE OF FRENCH
FRIES, BAKED POTATO OR RICE, FRESH GARDEN
SALAD (CHOICE OF DRESSING) ROLLS AND BUTTER

NEW ENGLAND CLAMBOIL . . .
Clams, fish, sausage, frankfurt, chourico, potato, onion served with
broth and drawn butter.

_____

"Addition of Lobster - extra charge."

DESSERTS

CHEESECAKE _____
New york style. Made with sour cream and cream cheese.

CHOCOLATE MOUSSE _____
Sinfully rich and chocolaty.

ICE CREAM _____

LOBSTER

"SEAWATER STEAM PROCESS"

Lobsters are brought to us daily from the Cold Atlantic Ocean by local boats. The natural sweetness and tenderness of our Lobsters are best preserved by our unique Seawater Steam Process.

Lobster weights listed are not exact, but are as close as nature will allow.

When ordering a larger lobster   1¼Lb., 1½Lb., 1¾Lb., 2Lb., 2½Lb. and 3Lb.
baked stuffed add $1.50   And are all priced according to
per half pound of stuffing.   Daily Market Price

MOBY DICK'S STEAMED LOBSTER   ◄ Market Price ►
Famous house specialty.

LOBSTER ON A BED OF CLAMS   ◄ Market Price ►
1¼LB. Lobster served with steamers and drawn butter.

BAKED STUFFED LOBSTER   ◄ Market Price ►
1½LB. Lobster baked with chef's own seafood stuffing.

BROILED LOBSTER   ◄ Market Price ►
1½LB. Lobster broiled with virgin olive oil and herbs.

LOBSTER PIE   ◄ Market Price ►
Fresh lobster chunks, in a sauce, topped with a puff pastry.

LOBSTER SAUTE   ◄ Market Price ►
Fresh sweet lobster chunks sauteed in butter, wine, and herbs.

SWORDFISH   ◄ Market Price ►
Grilled and served au natural or with caper butter.

BAKED STUFFED SHRIMP   _____
Jumbo shrimp baked in casserole with seafood stuffing.

BAKED STUFFED SOLE   _____
With seafood stuffing and tarragon cream sauce.

BAKED SCALLOP CASSEROLE   _____
With fresh dill and sherry butter.

SCROD   _____
Baked with white wine and lemon - also served with a herb crumb topping.

FRIED CLAMS   _____
Whole clams, fried golden brown, served with tartar sauce.

FRIED SEAFOOD PLATTER   _____
A sampling of the freshest fish, scallops, shrimp and clams served with tartar sauce.

MOBY DICK WHARF RESTAURANT
ON THE WATERFRONT

LUNCHEON MENU

APPETIZERS
ON THE HALF SHELL
LITTLE NECKS _____ OYSTERS _____
JUMBO SHRIMP _____
STEAMERS _____
Clean 'n sweet served with drawn butter
MUSSELS _____
Steamed in white wine, garlic and chopped tomato
CLAMS CASINO _____
Broiled with casino butter, topped with bacon
GRILLED SHRIMP SKEWER _____
with andouille sausage, peppers and whole mustard sauce
SMOKED CHICKEN AND FRUIT _____
Lightly smoked served with raspberry dressing
CLAM CAKES "AHAB'S FAMOUS"
½ Doz _____ 1 Doz _____
COLD SEAFOOD VARIETY _____
Two poached shrimp and scallops oyster salad with our mayonnaise
CAJUN POPCORN _____
Baby shrimp cajun style served with dipping sauce

CHOWDERS & SOUPS
MOBY DICK'S CLAM CHOWDER
Cup _____ Bowl _____
SOUP OF THE DAY _____

LUNCHEON PLATES
BROILED SCROD _____
FISH & CHIPS _____
FRIED SCALLOP PLATE _____
FRIED CLAM PLATE _____
LUNCHEON PLATES SERVED WITH FRENCH FRIES AND COLE SLAW

BEVERAGES
COFFEE _____
DECAF _____
TEA _____
JUICE _____
Orange, grapefruit, cranberry, pineapple and tomato

SANDWICH SELECTIONS
FRIED CLAMS _____
SCALLOPS _____
FRIED FISH _____
LOBSTER SALAD _____
TUNA SALAD _____
SEAFOOD SALAD _____

BURGERS
BASIC _____ MUSHROOM _____
CHEESE _____ BACON _____
GRILLED CHICKEN _____
SANDWICHES SERVED WITH POTATO CHIPS & PICKLE. ON ROLL OR SYRIAN.

HALF SANDWICHES
LOBSTER _____
TUNA _____
SEAFOOD _____
HALF SANDWICHES SERVED WITH CUP OF CHOWDER OR SOUP

SALAD PLATES
TUNA SALAD _____ SEAFOOD _____
LOBSTER SALAD _____
SERVED WITH SEASONAL GREENS AND VEGGIES

LOBSTERS
LOBSTER
"GUARANTEED STEAM PROCESS"
Lobsters are brought to us daily from the Cape Atlantic Ocean to our boats. Thy natural sweetness and tenderness of our Lobsters are best preserved by our unique Guaranteed Steam Process
Lobster weights listed are not exact, but are as close as nature will allow.
½LB, 1¼LB, 1½LB, 2LB, 2½LB and 3LB
And are all priced according to Daily Market Price
MOBY DICK'S STEAMED LOBSTER • Market Price •
Portion house specialty
1½LB, 1½LB, 1½LB, 2LB, 2½LB and 3LB

NEW ENGLAND CLAMBOIL
Clams, fish, sausage, frankfort potatoes, onions served with broth and drawn butter
"Addition of Lobster - extra charge"

DESSERTS

⑧ ⊙ Sharp as a Knife

Size matters they say, and that is certainly true of lobsters. Lobsters are affectionately known as bugs, which is actually what lobster larvae are called. In order for lobsters to meet the minimum requirements of a legal catch in Massachusetts, they must be at least 3.25 inches in length from the eye socket to the beginning of the tail (called the carapace or the body) and at least one pound. Any lobster that is less than the minimum size and weight is known as a short. At one pound they are called chicks and in Maine they cannot be smaller than ¾ of a pound in size. A lobster pot generally has three or four compartments, with holes in the netting large enough for shorts to escape from their captors ... only to postpone the inevitable.

Nearly two years after the great fire that destroyed the building on the water, it was time for the Moby Dick Restaurant to rise from the ashes. It was going to take pockets to resurrect the business and one of the new owners possessed those.

On May 20, 1993, Peter H. Sharp formed Winward Food Service Corp. and set a July 1 target date to open. He did not wish to miss the traffic of the summer months and he retained the name for the restaurant. As fate would have it, however, he did miss the summer traffic because he was unable to open until September 9. In actuality, Father-in-law Jackson Clemmey was not a financial partner in the operation but was referred to as one in the newspaper announcement.

The new owner set out to hire New Jersey architect Glenn Fries and local builder Bill Shaw to implement his plan. The construction was not major because the fire did not damage the entire building, thanks the efforts of Chief Bill Tripp and the volunteers of the Westport Fire Department. However, there was a need for a new kitchen. The east wall was moved out six inches to help improve the flow of the waitstaff from the kitchen to the dining area. While Shaw and his crew were at it, a new bar area was installed and a change was made to the seating configuration. The total cost exceeded $1.3 million. $100,000 of that amount was for kitchen equipment replacement. The current restaurant and owners are the beneficiaries of these investment made by Peter Sharp.

Since the establishment had been closed for two years, there was a need for a new staff. Sharp hired Eben Davis, the head chef from the exclusive Squantum Club in East Providence, Rhode Island, to be the executive chef. He soon became Peter Sharp's uncle by marriage. Michael Galvin, who had been trained by the Back Bay Group in Boston, admirably ran the front of the house, according to Chef Davis. Even into the cold, snowy month of January 1994, there was a two to four hour wait for a table on a Saturday night. Customers from as far as Boston found the ambiance, service, and impeccable food to their liking.

Sharp wanted the best and money was no object for the only son of an international financier and hotelier. He needed to invest $1 million in a new waste water system under ground on the site across the road to the south to conform to Massachusetts state law regulations at the time. The two large holding tanks were required to be pumped on a daily basis and, due to the lack of an on-site well, tanker trucks also needed to frequently deliver fresh water to the site. Some said his wealth caused him to be cautious and skeptical of other people's motives.

Peter Jay Sharp Sr. died in 1992, more than a year before his son, Peter Jr. purchased the Moby Dick. Peter Jay Sharp Sr. owned the famous Carlyle Hotel, known informally as The Carlyle. It is a combination luxury and residential hotel located at 35 East 76th Street on the northeast corner of Madison Avenue, in the Upper East Side of New York City. The hotel is designed in Art Deco style and was named after Scottish essayist Thomas Carlyle.

Owned since 2001 by Rosewood Hotels & Resorts, The Carlyle is a cooperative with 180 rental rooms and suites and sixty privately owned residences. With hotels in London as well as New York City,

Peter Jay Sharp was reportedly worth more than $1 billion at the time of his passing.

Forty-year-old Peter H. Sharp maintained a residence a short drive away from his waterfront restaurant on Main Road on Westport Point. His neighbors dubbed him the "Mayor of Westport," which was a title levied upon various residents at times within the community, which does not elect a mayor but is run by a five-member board of selectmen, who each serve three year terms.

On the final night before it changed to Sharp's ownership, with Nancy Kitchen again acting as a waitress, a local band entertained the clientele. The Funky White Honkies had them dancing through the entire building with their upbeat music. The floor dropped six inches but the sale went on—the building was propped up by caissons (a watertight retaining structure that is constructed so that the water can be pumped out, keeping the working environment dry), and the closing took place.

Sharp reportedly purchased the restaurant for access to the long deep-water dock. He hired a dock-boy to oversee the comings and goings of his own boats—a forty-foot sport fisherman and, later, an eighty-foot Concordia sailboat—and those of his restaurant guests. He did not serve food or beverages on the dock. It was used solely for visiting yachts. An avid boatman, he wanted to own the dock as a way to access his own vessel.

One of Sharp's political acquaintances sailed into the harbor one day and landed at his dock and was to be joined by others for dinner. Apparently, he did not tip the dock-boy but autographed menus instead. When his group gathered to eat, they ordered the top shelf wines for dinner and desert. The house paid for the entire meal and the two servers who worked the Captain's Room went home tipless at the end of the night.

But that was not the end of the story.

After closing on a Sunday it was necessary to take inventory and clean the building. There was then a loud banging on the locked door. Back came the now well-known politician in a wet bathing suit that was full of sand. "Let me in, I want to clean off and use your bathroom." Staff had orders to keep everyone out after closing time so they stuck to the rules. He said he did not want to dirty his clean boat and was told by staff that he was not going to dirty their clean bathroom either. Off sailed "Mr. don't-you-know-who-I-am," never to return. The staff stuck to their guns the following day when Sharp confronted them about the incident and the cost of the check the previous night. They told their boss that they were just following the rules Sharp had laid down after some priceless scrimshaw he owned displayed had been stolen one winter night. Sharp then authorized a twenty percent tip for the two servers on the $2,500 check that his pal had rung up. So went the profits for that weekend!

Sharp continued the menu of seafood and even lowered the prices a bit. As the years went by, the prices did rise to best reflect the cost of goods. The facility retained its seafood menu but more almond crusted cod was sold than lobstahs. He discovered that serving lunch with sandwiches, chowdah, and steamers was not enough to keep the wolf away from the door. Current owners have learned from this and no longer serve lunch or solely maintain slips on the dock for visitors.

For years the Mody Dick has rented slips to local sailors. At one point, they granted a slip to a local who had been evicted from two other docks, but the owners provided him here with a three strike policy. That was all well and good until a visiting sailor pulled into the rented slip. There were physical fireworks to follow and the new owner requested the slip owner vacate the premises immediately. The visitors got a free meal from the owner and a black eye as a result of the skirmish.

After Sharp let Michael Galvin go, he conducted a search for a new house manager. He found her, Cheryl, within earshot across the harbor, working in her husband's lobstah business. He also employed John Panchley as an assistant front of the house manager.

The restaurant continued to flourish under Eben's cooking. It was a restaurant of distinction, impeccable, just like it is today. Young Brian Corey (now an attorney in town and represents the present ownership) served a great drink at the bar and the corporation decided to purchase the former Moby Dick Sandwich Shop across the road to the south, operated by nearby resident Lido Jerome. Sharp renamed it Strippers, which was also open for lunch and dinner but only had a beer and wine license and not a full liquor license. The more casual atmosphere at Strippers drew a nearly full house of locals nightly, with full liquor glasses transported from the Back Eddy bar across the street to the north.

During this timeframe, Sharp arranged for a water taxi to transport patrons from the Spindle Rock dock in Westport Harbor or from a moored boat in the Harbor to the restaurant dock. The price was $2 per head, round trip, plus tip for the operator. The power driven skiff could accommodate six or seven people at most and it was highly popular in its early stages. It was an answer to the problem of drinking and driving—by car or boat. But this service was not solely a generous gesture on Sharp's part—it allowed patrons to consume more beverages without the fear of an accident.

The taxi driver was responsible but it is doubtful that any insurance company would look favorably on the practice. Patrons would take the last taxi of the night at 10:00 p.m. but many would still need to drive their cars home. As the crow flies from Spindle Rock Club in Westport Harbor near the mouth of the ocean it takes ten minutes to reach the Back Eddy Dock, but by auto it is a good twenty minutes on back roads that have more twists and turns than the old Comet roller coaster at Lincoln Park. After Sharp gave up the service it was assumed, temporarily, by Tripp's Boat yard, but they gave up that aspect of their business in no time flat.

Six years later, in 1999, Sharp decided to sell the business and moved to Providence, Rhode Island.

It was time for a new owner with a new name to come aboard.

⊙ Schlesinger's Time

Lobsters are particular about what they eat. They prefer to catch and kill their own food such as fish, mollusk, vegetable matter, and early stage plankton.

Chris Schlesinger entered the food industry at age eighteen when he dropped out of college to become a restaurant dishwasher. He loved the fast-paced work in a kitchen so he decided to pursue a career in the culinary business. This Virginia native became a line cook and developed a love for barbecue, spicy food, and live fire cooking. In 1977, he graduated from the Culinary Institute of America (CIA) and worked with some of New England's most innovative chefs, prior to opening his own place in 1985—the East Coast Grill in Cambridge, Massachusetts. It closed its doors in late January of 2016 after a thirty year run. Jason Heard operated it at the time it shuttered.

The exceptionally harsh winter of 2015 was credited as the main reason for the closing. When the Grill did close it did so with a bang—another Hell Night. There was hot stuff a-plenty to eat, and patrons, known as Chilli-Heads, enjoyed every bite. On the last night, the owner brought back the hottest dishes from past decades such as Pasta from Hell to serve to the faithful. Reports from the *Boston Globe* said they loved it.

The co-author of seven cookbooks and winner of the James Beard Cookbook Award, Schlesinger is also a teacher at the Culinary Institute of America in New York and California, and was the chef at the nearby Sakonnet Country Club in Little Compton, Rhode Island.

Chris Schlesinger.
Photo courtesy of Wikipedia.

Prior to owning a summer home near Buzzards Bay in Westport, Schlesinger worked in thirty-five different restaurants that featured grilling and seafood. By 1999, Schlesinger decided to consolidate his efforts at multiple establishments and focused his attention on the East Coast Grill. But he needed a summer endeavor, which he found less than a mile from his summer place on the water.

He quickly established working relationships with local fishermen, farmers, vintners, brewers, and cheese makers. Those relationships are still in place today. Schlesinger's partners were Sal Liotta, who had never been to the town prior to this, and Saul Garlick, who specialized in accounting for restaurants in the Boston area.

On December, 17, 1998, Schlessinger and his partners ventured down to Bridge Street, found an empty establishment on the Westport River with hardly any food or beverages in stock, took a one year lease with three additional five year options, and called the restaurant The Back Eddy.

A friend, Attorney Dan George, had noticed that the river to the northeast, near the rock formations, flowed counterclockwise to the main stream in an eddy fashion, and so it was named. True to its name, The Back Eddy was conceived as a seafood restaurant that does things a little bit differently.

Dan George, who is now retired, was the owner of what was called the Moby Dick Sandwich Shop, later The Way Back Eddy. The business is now Smoke and Pickles Catering. George sold that business to three staff members who currently operate the catering business. Lido Jerome owned the land where the sandwich shop was located and there was an easement in the deed for the well point. This land provided The Back Eddy with its consumable water.

Jerome was known to be an unpleasant local who spent considerable money and time in a Back Eddy bar booth. After a few drinks, his attitude and always-surly behavior turned mean from the Scotch whisky. He was known to hold grudges to the extreme. As an example, at some point Jerome decided to amend the easement and inserted the provision that if anyone named Tripp purchased the property that the easement would cease to apply. The name Tripp in Westport is as common as Smith in other parts of the country and even until his passing no one, including his wife, who revoked the amendment after his death, knew which Tripp he was so upset at.

Schlesinger hired a sous chef named Aaron deRego, who is today one of the owners, and with the help of the chef from East Coast Grill they set up shop. By April 1, 1999 they started to remodel. They retained the open kitchen concept and the flooring but began replacing furniture, including the oriental rugs, which made the dining area very dark. They also leased The Poor Farm on Drift Road as dormitory housing for the non-local kitchen help. As they made physical changes, it was necessary to work through the landlord's designee, Rob Kiley, to approve items for payment in behalf of Windwood Food Corp. Oftentimes local craftspeople were slow in delivery, which was due to the previous owner's payment schedule that could be from six months to a full year in the arrears. Team Schlesinger paid $10,000 per month in year-round rent despite the abbreviated season.

They rehired former manager Cheryl Gifford to run the operation. During the interview process, the restaurant was undergoing various cosmetic improvements. The dining area and entranceway floors were being varnished and no one was allowed to walk on them. But Cheryl had scheduled an interview with Chris on the second floor in the office. There was only one way to get there. Cheryl climbed onto the outside roof, entered through a window and, with that type of determination, was soon on the payroll.

The 1999 first season was nearly a disaster. Prior to opening the door, all liquor distributors needed to be paid in full, as Sharp had let those payments become delinquent. The chef from Cambridge was accustomed to serving entrees to an eighty-seat capacity facility. The Back Eddy could seat 240. It sometimes took one hour and sixteen minutes from the time an order was placed to when it was served. Most orders were, as anticipated, for lobstah in some form and that left Chris and Sal spending each night apologizing to customers for the long wait. They would announce to customers that there was good news and bad news—dinner is almost out but it will be another ten minutes. Lobstah pasta was the main time consuming culprit and the kitchen and chef were not properly prepared to move that item in a timely basis out of the kitchen to the hungry patrons. If it were not for the quality of the meals and Schlesinger's reputation many patrons would never have come back.

"When we first opened up the Back Eddy, we would all jump in the river at the end of the night," reported long-time waitress Karen Walsh, whose three daughters, Sarah, Hannah, and Caroline have joined her on staff over the years. "We were hot and busy throughout the night so we would just jump in, fully-clothed, and then go back to work [cleaning up]. One night I remember being especially busy and just couldn't wait for the end of the shift, so we just jumped in, fully-clothed, got out, put our shoes back on, and went right back to waiting on guests [dripping wet]. One year Chris [Schlesinger] installed a diving board. We enjoyed that for awhile until it was taken down, probably because he feared that someone would get hurt," concluded Karen.

The restaurant had its regulars, some of whom were elderly and forgetful. They often left without paying their bills. Happily this mistake would never become a charge-off because family members would periodically come in and resolve any unpaid bills for them.

Over the years, the waitstaff created games to play while on duty, like The Buzzard Game, which included a Buzzards Bay Brewing sticker on the person who was IT. If you wore the sticker at the end of the night, you paid a visit to the river, fully-clothed. Oftentimes, this staff person in the river was quickly followed by customers.

A bridal party member was once spotted in the kitchen celebrating with the back of the house staff. Customers often joined in the fun with staff at the end of the night. It is tradition that at summer's end staff would end up in the river for a final dunking. But care had to be taken when driving home for both staff and patrons, especially on a foggy night. Patrons and servers have both been known to take a sharp left coming out of the parking lot and, instead of ending up on Route 88 heading back north, drove straight into the river via the boat ramp. Perhaps, it was one too many grappa's that influenced the drivers ability to focus.

In the end, Schlesinger found his summer escape to Westport was anything but. He found himself at the restaurant rather than enjoying his home near the water. It became time to sell his shares to his partners— Aaron, the chef and Sal, the manager.

And so, at the end of the decade it was time for another chapter in the history of Westport's long-time, and only, waterfront restaurant.

Entrees

Grilled Double-Thick Peppered Tuna Steak... with Pickled Ginger, Soy, Wasabi, Asian Slaw, Grilled Vegetables & Grilled Sweet Potato — 22.00

Grilled Salmon Filet... with a Tomato Ginger Chutney, Grilled Asparagus & a Cous-Cous Raisin Salad — 19.00

Roasted Codfish... with Tomatoes, Kalomata Olives & Artichoke Hearts, served with Parsley Potatoes & Garlic Seared Spinach — 18.00

Bob & Cheryl's "Naked" Leos Wharf Lobster... 1.5 lb. or 2.5 lb. — market

Westport Shore Dinner... 1.5 lb Lobster, 2 lb of Steamers, Chourico, Local Corn, New Potatoes & Sweet Onions — 39.00

Fish & Chips... Best & Freshest. with Hand-Cut Fries, Eddy Slaw & House Tartar — 14.00

Fried New Bedford Scallops... with Hand-Cut Fries, Eddy Slaw & House Tartar — 17.00

Chippy's Style Fried Platter... Shrimp, Scallops & Cod with Hand-Cut Fries, Eddy Slaw & House Tartar — 21.00

Lobster Pasta... Fettucine tossed with Chunks of Lobster, Roasted Tomatoes, Asparagus & a Rich Creamy Corn & Lobster Sauce — 21.00

Bouillabaisse... Shrimp, Scallops, Mussels & Crispy Cod in a Tomato Fennel Broth — 23.00

Spicy Eddy Spaghetti... tossed with Garlic Steamed Mussels & Sausage in an Angry Tomato Sauce with Garlic Toast — 15.00

1 lb Grilled Peppered NY Sirloin Steak... with a Red Onion Jam, Grilled Veg, Ferolbink Farms Mashed Potatoes & Braised Garlic — 23.00

Back Eddy Vegetation Experience... including but not limited to: Grilled Vegetables, Asian Slaw, Garlic Spinach, Local Tomato & Corn Salad, Garlic Mashed Potatoes, Asparagus, Various Chutneys & Relishes, Grilled Garlic Bread & More! — 14.00

The Marcy... Arugula, Corn, Local Tomatoes & a Chipotle Vinaigrette with choice of a Peppered Sirloin Skewer or Grilled Basil Marinated Chicken — 12.00

Sandwiches
All served with Hand-Cut Fries, Eddy Slaw & Dan's House Pickles

Fish O' the Day... with House Tartar — 7.50

1/4 lb Eddy Burger — 6.50

Cheddar Cheese Burger — 7.50

NC Pulled Pork... with a Vinegar Sauce — 7.50

Traditional Lobster Roll... on a Toasted Pop — 12.50

Orange Marinated Grilled Chicken Sandwich... with Chipotle Mayo — 7.50

Side Dishes

Hand-Cut Fries	4.00	Grilled Veg or Dan's Pickles	4.00
Garlic Braised Mashed	4.00	Grandma's Baked Beans	3.00
Potato Salad	4.00	Cornbread	2.00

Your Chefs: Aaron Derego, Nigel Vincent & Brian Rebello

From Our Local Raw Bar

We are very proud of our shellfish & have cultivated relationships
with a few of New England's most conscientious growers & harvesters...

½ Dozen Oysters... (Very Stressed) on the ½ Shell	10.50
½ Dozen Littleneck Clams... on the ½ Shell	7.50
Colossal Shrimp Cocktail... Shell On	2.50/each
Cracked Local Rock Crab Claws	2.50/each
Eddy Raw Bar Platter...	45.00
with 1 Dozen Oysters, ½ Dozen Littlenecks, 4 Colossal Shrimp & 4 Crab Claws	

Soups, Salads & Appetizers

Westport River Clam & Roasted Corn Chowder... with Fresh Sage & Crackers	5.00
Manhattan Style Smoked Cod Chowder... with Sweet Potato & Croutons	5.00
Big Local Green Salad...with a Simple Balsamic Vinaigrette	4.50
Wild Arugula Salad... Grilled Peaches, Peppers, Olives & a Balsamic Vinaigrette	6.50
Eddy Salad... Eva's Greens, Coll's Tomatoes, "Great Hill" Blue, EVOO & Balsamic	7.50
Bowl O' Maine Steamers... with Drawn Butter & Fresh Clam Broth	market
Steamed Mussels ECG Style... with Coconut Milk, Ginger & Chiles	8.00
Peel & Eat Buffalo Shrimp... Great Southern Shrimp with Blue Cheese & Celery	9.50
Eddy Style Stuffed Clams... 3, with Chourico, Corn, Fresh Breadcrumbs & a Chili Aioli	5.50
House Smoked BBQ'd Salmon... served warm with Chili Mustard, Sweet Onion Marmalade & Cornbread Toast	8.50
# 1 Tuna Sashimi... with Arugula, Seaweed, Cucumber & a Soy Sesame Dressing	8.00

BBQ Platters

Cooked Low & Slow over Oak Smoke & served with
Eddy Slaw, Grandma's Baked Beans, Cornbread & Watermelon

Memphis Style Dry Rubbed Pork Ribs... with Sweet BBQ Sauce	14.00
North Carolina Style Pulled Pork... with a Vinegar Sauce	13.00
BBQ Rubbed ¼ Chicken... with All Southern BBQ Rub	12.00
Trio... all 3 !	16.00

Kid Stuff

Served with a Kid Beverage

Kid Pasta... with Butter & Cheese	6.00
Chicken Fingers... with Hand-Cut Fries & Eddy Slaw	6.00
Fish & Chips... with Hand-Cut Fries & Eddy Slaw	6.00

Wines by The Glass...Please ask us for a taste !

Sparkling Cava for our Local Raw Bar

NV	Mont~Marcal Brut Cava, Penedes, Spain	5.00

Glass White Wines

NV	Sakonnet "Eye of the Storm", Little Compton, Rhode Island	6.00
1999	Okhimney Creek Sauvignon Blanc, Marlborough, New Zealand	5.00
1998	Domaine Foulley, Chardonnay, Burgundy, France	6.00
1999	Borgo Magredo, Pinot Grigio, Friuli, Italy	6.00

Glass Red Wines

1997	Bandiera, Cabernet Sauvignon, Sonoma, California	5.00
1998	Chateau De Castelneau, Merlot, Bordeaux, France	6.00
1996	Caves des Papes, Cotes Du Rhone, Vaucluse, France	7.00

Beers (* = on tap)

* Buzzards Bay Brewing Co ~ Ask about Today's Selections (USA)	3.25
* Coors Light (USA)	2.75
* Guinness Stout (Ireland)	3.75
Amstel Light (Holland)	3.25
Budweiser Tall Boy, 16oz Can (USA)	3.00
Corona Extra (Mexico)	3.25
Heineken (Holland)	3.25
Mike's Hard Lemonade (USA)	3.25
Red Stripe Lager (Jamaica)	3.50
Sam Adams I.P.A. (USA)	3.50
Sierra Nevada Summerfest (USA)	3.50
O'Doul's Amber Non-Alcololic Brew (USA)	2.75
"Regular Guy" Beer Special: Narragansett, 16oz Can (USA)	2.75

From the Mixology Staff at the Bar... Margarita's & More...

Eddy Traditional... with Sauza Hornitos Tequila & Triple Sec	5.00
Blue Margarita... a Chris Favorite... with Cuervo 1800 & Blue Curacao	5.50
Melon Margarita... with Cuervo Gold, Midori & Fresh Squeezed Sour Mix	5.50
One Eyed Jake... with Patron, Grand Marnier & Fresh Squeezed Sour Mix	6.50
Mangorita... with El Jimador Agave, Blue Curacao & Fresh Mango	6.00
Mezcal Margarita... with Monte Alban Mezcal & Bacardi Tropico	6.00
Dark & Stormy... Goslings Dark Rum, Ginger Beer & a Squeeze of Lime	6.00
Sangria... Traditional Rojo or Tropical Blanco	3.00/glass or 9.00/pitcher

Fresh Squeezed Juices & Other Stuff

Fresh Squeezed Orange & Grapefruit Juices... the Juice & Nothin' Else	2.50
Coke, Sprite, Diet Coke, Ginger Ale & Fanta Orange... with Free Refills	1.75
IBC Cream Soda, IBC Root Beer, Stephan's Ginger Beer	2.50
Mango Iced Tea, Fresh Squeezed Lemonade	2.25
H2O, 250ml... Pellegrino Sparkling or Evian Still	1.75

Kitchen Appreciation Pitcher

Now You Can Buy The Hardest Working
Kitchen Staff on The Planet
A Pitcher of Fresh Buzzards Bay Beer
$9.00

And Now...The Fine Print

◆ The Back Eddy is open Year Round – Ask about our seasonal hours

◆ We take reservations for Parties of 6 or more - on a limited basis

◆ Special Menus are available for Parties of 12 or more

◆ The Back Eddy is available for private & semi-private events,
for groups of any size

◆ We use some pretty wild ingredients here, so please let us know if
you have any food allergies

◆ If you bring in your own cake we charge $1.50 per person plate charge

◆ We accept Cash, Amex, Visa, Mastercard or Discover – Sorry no Checks

◆ For your convenience, for parties of 6 or more, we automatically add
an 18% gratuity

◆ Because of the complexity of our dishes & the volume of our
summer business – no substitutions please !

Thanks

Thanks for joining us today! We truly appreciate your coming by
& if any part of your visit did not meet with your expectations,
please let someone on the staff know so we can try to do better!

Your Hosts: Chris Schlesinger & Sal Liotta

---

check us out on the web at
www.TheBackEddy.I.Am

The Back Eddy Days

Lobster shells were once used to make golf balls. After processing, the shells were discarded into landfills. By recycling the shells, the belief was that something could be made of them—as well as keeping the proceeds in the lobster industry. A University of Maine professor created golf balls with lobster shells as the core. The ball had some positives—it was biodegradable and designed for hitting off cruise ships or on courses with lakes and oceans. The negative was that they would only travel seventy percent the distance of a regular ball, so they will not be part of any PGA tour event soon.

Many changes have occurred in the physical structure to the old Moby Dick restaurant. Pilings have been added over the years, to a current total of forty-eight, providing more support to the facility. But one unique aspect has remained consistent: The opening traps in the floor still allow the rising river water during extra high tides to stabilize the building and keep it safe. This design proved extremely beneficial during Hurricane Bob in 1991 and during extraordinary high tides, which seem to be happening with more frequency over recent years. Luckily, there haven't been any major storms to again test the effectiveness of the traps. Liota notes, however, that the river has been rising over the past few years compared to the 1990s when he first ran the dining facility.

The restaurant was reconfigured for efficiency and the present owners rehabed the bar and kitchen. The oriental rugs have been removed as have the whale oil lamps, but the present table and chairs remain, thanks to the generosity of the Sharp family. They are now twenty years old and still look like new.

The Back Eddy Restaurant (*photo from the website*).

At one point there were lights strung under the dock into the river but the electrical fears were too great to allow them to remain.

The outside beverage bar as well as the raw bar and grill are still busy on the docks. On Sunday afternoons, a band provides sunset music and creates a festive atmosphere from 4:00 to 8:00 p.m.

For the past seventeen years, the restaurant has sponsored an annual fall season Stripped Bass Fishing Tournament. As many as 150 participants, in multiple divisions, join the event as they head to the ocean for the catch. There are ten prizes, with a grand prize of $500 for the largest fish caught over the four-day event. It is not just an event for the locals and, in fact, many summer folk return to cast their luck in the waters of Buzzards Bay. The final day of the long weekend tournament is highlighted by an engraved trophy presentation and a buffet with bass and blue fish cooked a dozen different ways. Event participants are presented with T-shirts, many have all seventeen, and various prizes are given away by restaurant vendors. All involved look forward to this yearly competition and food extravaganza.

The final event before the season ends in January is the New Year's Day Polar Plunge, which is a salute to Westport locals. Young and old, single people and families, show up on the dock and try to stay warm before and after the swim. No wet suits are allowed for the approximately 200 brave souls who are encouraged in their adventure by a similar number of cheering onlookers. One year, the outside temperature hit a balmy 57 degrees and nearly 450 people showed up to jump.

One year, however, no one could participate because the cold temperatures froze the water around the docks. If a patron jumps into the cold water and gets their hair wet, they are awarded with a free buffet lunch, oftentimes served by Cory Gifford, a great-granddaughter of the original owners, Sheldon and Evelyn Judson, or Andee Manchester, the daughter of one of the orginal waitreeses.

Many of the current staff has been working at the restaurant for years: bartenders Tanya Martin and Megan Alves and waiter Joey Michaels. These folks and others have brought along family to work at the restaurant, like Karen Walsh and her three daughters. There are eighty-seven employees and fifty of that number have been on staff for ten or more years.

The New Year's Day party is loud and raucous, according to Liotta. On New Year's Day, 2016, 175 patrons had made reservations and another hundred walk-ins were expected. Most were young people who came for the excitement and the free buffet lunch, like the members of the Portsmouth Swim Club who shared the warmth of the heat blower in the main room after their dunk.

"Oh, my feet are frozen," one was heard saying.

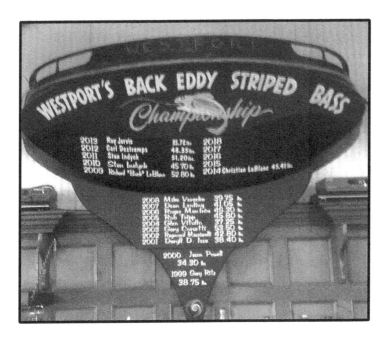

Owners Aaron de Rego and Sal Liotta pose in the kitchen
on New Years Day 2016.

Some adults arrived in bathing suits covered by terry-cloth robes
for warmth before and after their jump. Members of the faithful Vikings
Motorcycle Club (twenty-four strong) also participated. Entire families
also joined in the fun, like the Woltman family of Westport, formerly
of Fall River. Grandfather Lee stayed warm in his winter jacket while
family members Brian Parylak (fifth time participating) and daughter
Gwyneth, age ten, and Jack Woltman age nineteen, joined in the fun.
The water and air temperatures were both in the mid-forties, making
the jump less of a shock to the system, some say.

Unlike a chain restaurant, Liotta feels that the local community has
a vested social interest in the restaurant. It is a place "where everyone
knows your name," comes in to meet and greet neighbors and friends,
and relaxes with a good meal.

One evening, a local community leader was having a beverage with
the wife of another well-known patron. A simple telephone call from
someone in the establishment led to the husband coming in and feeling
humorless. After a barrage of four-letter words, the husband ordered

a shot of whisky. The woman quickly departed and the two men sat together and enjoyed a glass of wine.

Very rarely has there ever been a brawl or even fisticuffs.

The average check today is $55 per diner. And on a busy day in August it takes only thirty-six minutes to serve the 800-plus customers. Chef/owner Aaron says they should not be serving so fast because patrons will think the restaurant wants to move them out quickly—and that is the farthest thing from the truth. The restaurant's motto is simplicity, not speed.

Both the bar and the menu are based upon the concept of simple and top of the line delivery. The bar, on the other hand, provides quick service and only makes a few specialty drinks, like Margaritas and Bloody Marys, because speed is critical to making bar customers satisfied. If a customer has to wait too long for a beverage they can become frustrated, so simple execution is a standard.

Jack Woltman, Gwyneth and Dad, Brian Parylak
tries to stay warm after the plunge

Entire families like the Russell's join together
after the plunge for a sumptuous buffet.

Dinner plates do not serve hot side dishes in order to keep the kitchen functioning at maximum efficiency. The meal consists of a starch, a protein, and a cold vegetable. The menu has remained constant over the years in the summer due to the customer desires. Many patrons in the summer are area renters and visit the town for only two weeks at a time. They come for certain meals and return yearly with the same request. Of course, lobstahs remain one of the top items on the menu. Friday night sees many visitors who attend the outdoor concerts at the Westport Vineyards up the road and complete the evening at the restaurant. The spring and fall permits the kitchen to change the menu and serve other options to the steady year-round customers.

Serving local food is also key to the long-term success of the establishment. Lobstahs and oysters come from nearby Sakonnet, Rhode Island, and Shy Brothers Cheese comes from less than a mile away on Main Road. Westport Vineyards supplies wine and Buzzards Bay Brewery sells craft beers to the facility. Mello's Chourico in nearby Fall River supplies Portuguese food products for the restaurant.

The owners strongly feel that they have an obligation to the community. They feel that they are the caretakers of this long-standing enterprise that provides both employment opportunities and dining pleasure in an area that has a limited number of each.

The private rooms allow for special occasion gatherings, like celebrating the start of the summer with a grappa party. At the conclusion of a wonderful meal, the owners might send in a complimentary bottle of grappa for the revelers.

The strong after-dinner liqueur could easily tilt one over the edge, as it did early one summer night to one lady. As she and her husband drove home (he did not partake) she urged him to pull over on the bridge on route 88 so that she could cleanse her system. As she hung out of the side door of the car, one of her friends, who was driving by, spotted her. He waited until the next day to call her Rhode Island home and asked to speak with her under the pretense that the caller was a Westport authority person who had spotted her ill health cooking on the roadway and demanded that she return to clean up the mess she had made or be subject to arrest.

No more grappa for her!

Restaurants often fail because too many owners use the business as a playground and take to drinking the profits or carousing with the staff. For The Back Eddy, formerly The Moby Dick, the beat goes on.

This restaurant has been a Westport landmark for over a half-century. With many more years ahead for The Back Eddy, you can rest assured that lobstah will be available and new stories will be added to the history of this important local eatery.

The Back Eddy Restaurant

Our Name

When we first opened The Back Eddy, one of our biggest challenges was: what to name the restaurant? What name would reflect our philosophy & cooking style?

The name itself actually came from a dear friend of ours who defined a "back eddy" as a current that runs counter clockwise to the mainstream. This defines our restaurant perfectly. A seafood restaurant that does things a little bit differently.

Vision

Our mission is to promote eating locally produced product. We feel fortunate to be located at the center of so many food traditions. This area enjoys a rich heritage of working people growing, raising & catching food, as well as preparing it with a mix of culinary traditions.

The ultra fresh produce from the many farms of Southeastern Massachusetts & Coastal Rhode Island; the wide variety of fish brought to shore by New England's Fisherman; wine, beer, & cheese from local artisan producers & the mixture of Portuguese influence with the oldest American cooking style, provides our kitchen with an incredibly diverse range to work with.

We are excited to help our community sustain growth by providing our local farmers & fisherman a place to showcase their talents.

With our concept of thinking coastal & eating local we can provide you, our guests, with the freshest food in the area. Hence our name and why it is so important to us.

We thank the best staff on the planet, our guests and our suppliers, for helping to support our vision.

Location

We are located on the Westport River in beautiful Southcoast Massachusetts. Our restaurant has a fabulous waterfront view, boat access, and is moments away from the beaches. In addition to our main dining rooms and bar area, during the summer weekends we also have an outdoor bar, raw bar & grille on the dock!

More info

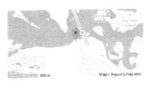

Westport Point, MA

Get the 10 day forecast

Severe Weather
Airport Delays
Beach Conditions
Pollen Reports

69 °F
Cloudy

Feels Like: 69°F
Humidity: 83%
Wind: E at 17 mph
Enter City/zip

Keeping an eye on the Tropics

83 people like this. Be the first of your friends.

500 m   Map © Report a map error

75

When we first opened The Back Eddy,
one of our biggest challenges was: what to name the restaurant?
What name would reflect our philosophy & cooking style?
The name itself actually came from a dear friend of ours who defined a
"back eddy" as current that runs counter clockwise to the mainstream.
This defines our restaurant perfectly:
A seafood restaurant that does things a little bit differently.
Our mission is to promote eating locally produced product.
We feel fortunate to be located at the center of so many food traditions.
The Farm Coast enjoys a rich heritage of working people growing, raising,
& catching food, as well as preparing it with a mix of culinary traditions.

The Back Eddy

The ultra fresh produce from the many farms of
Southeastern Massachusetts & Coastal Rhode Island;
the wide variety of fish brought to shore by New England's Fisherman;
wine, beer, & cheese from local artisan producers & the mixture of
Portuguese influence with the oldest American cooking style,
provides our kitchen with an incredibly diverse range to work with.
We are excited to help our community sustain growth by providing
our local farmers & fisherman a place to showcase their talents.
With our concept of thinking coastal & eating local
we can provide you, our guests, with the freshest food in the area.
Hence our name and why it is so important to us.
As we move into our 17th season,
we thank the best staff on the planet, our guests & our suppliers,
for helping to support our vision.

Raw Bar...All Local, All The Time

*½ Dozen Sakonnet Oysters... with a cranberry mignonette	14.00
*½ Dozen Native Littlenecks... with fresh cocktail sauce & lemon	10.50
4 Giant Wild White Shrimp Cocktail... with cocktail sauce & lemon	14.00
*Mini Raw Bar Platter... 3 oysters, 3 little necks & 2 shrimp	18.50

cocktail sauce "from hell" available...ask your server !!!

Soups, Starters & Salads

Back Eddy Signature Roasted Corn & Clam Chowder... with fresh herbs, apple wood bacon & arruda's fresh cream	7.50
Super Fresh Soup of the Moment... ask your server!	mkt
3 Eddy Signature Stuffed Clams... with mello's chourico, roasted corn & tabasco aioli	8.50
Steamed PEI Mussels... with a spicy marinara & garlic bread	11.50
Citrus Cured Salmon... with cloumage, micro greens & crusty bread	9.50
Salted Cod & Potato Cakes... with an onion relish	9.50
Native Steamers... with real butter & lemon	mkt
Deviled Eggs from Hell... with an inner beauty drizzle	9.00
Wood Grilled Flatbread... with roasted butternut squash, cloumage, sage, pinenuts & EVOO	10.50
Tomato Braised Boneless Short Rib... with house made gnocci & shaved pecorino romano	10.50
Local Greens Salad... with a sherry vinaigrette	7.50
Eddy Salad...with arugula, candied pecans, sliced apple, great hill blue cheese & a cider vinaigrette	8.50

*This item is raw or partially cooked & can increase your risk of illness.
Consumers who are especially vulnerable to food borne illness should only
eat seafood & other foods from animals thoroughly cooked

Sandwiches

all served with hand-cut fries, eddy slaw & house pickles

Fried Fish... with tartar	10.50
¼# Angus Hot Dog... with spicy mustard	8.00
Pulled Pork... north carolina style	10.00

Kid Stuff ~ 12 & Under !

all served with a kid beverage & a hoodsie cup

Chicken Tenders... with hand-cut fries	9.00
Fish & Chips... with hand-cut fries & still nick's tartar	10.50
¼# Hot Dog... with hand-cut fries	8.00
Mac & Cheese... with cheddar	8.50

Your Chefs & Hosts:
Aaron DeRego, Nigel Vincent,
Soda Phan,
Sal Liotta & Michelle Tripp

Sorry if you missed it...
Brunch !
Every Sunday after Columbus Day, we serve Sunday Brunch from 11am to 2pm!
Best Bloody Mary Ever!!!

White

	btl	gl
2007 Westport Rivers "RJR Brut" Sparkling, Westport, MA *sparkling*	50	10
N.V. Taittinger, Brut La Francaise, Champagne, France	86	
2004 Moet et Chandon, "Cuvee Dom Perignon", Champagne, France	228	
2013 Long Lake Cellars, Chardonnay, Napa, California *fruity & crisp*	28	7
2014 Columna, Albarino, Rias Baixas, Spain	30	
2014 Villa San Martino, Pinot Grigio, Venezia, Italy	32	8
2014 Greenstone Point, Sauvignon Blanc, Marlborough, New Zealand	34	
2013 Westport Rivers, Chardonnay, Down The Block, Massachusetts	36	
2013 Zum, Riesling, Mosel, Germany *spicy & aromatic*	32	
2014 Durnberg, Gruner Veltliner, Falkenstein, Austria	34	
2013 Waterbrook, Pinot Gris, Walla Walla, Washington State	36	9
2014 Round Pond, Sauvignon Blanc, Napa, California	40	10
2012 Henri Bourgeois, Sancerre, Loire Valley, France	46	
2013 Antonutti, Pinot Grigio, Friuli, Italy *luscious & rich*	36	
2014 Bourgeois, Petite Sauvignon, Loire, France	40	
2013 Noble Tree, Chardonnay, Chalk Hill-Russian River, California	44	11
2012 Larochette, Pouilly Fuisse, Burgundy, France	48	12
2013 Cakebread, Chardonnay, Napa, California	56	

Today's Selections

	btl	g
N.V. Primaterra, Prosecco, Vicentino, Italy	32	8
2014 Brampton, "Unoaked" Chardonnay, Western Cape, South Africa	40	10
2012 Hook & Ladder, Cabernet Sauvignon, Russian River Valley, California	44	11

Red

	btl	gl
2013 Luc Pirlet, Merlot, Languedoc, France *smooth & elegant*	28	7
2011 Fleur Du Cap, Merlot, Stellenbosch, South Africa	30	
2013 Vinalba, Malbec, Mendoza, Argentina	32	8
2013 Maurelle, Cotes Du Rhone, Rhone, France	36	
2013 Alchemist, Pinot Noir, Willamette Valley, Oregon	42	
2013 Mas de Gourgonnier, Les Baux, Provence, France *earthy & spicy*	34	
2013 Wolf Blass, Cabernet Sauvignon, Adelaide, Australia	36	9
2013 Sharecropper's, Cabernet Sauvignon, Prosser, Washington State	38	
2011 Hedges, CMS, Columbia Valley, Washington State	40	10
2013 Ken Wright, Pinot Noir, Willamette Valley, Oregon	48	
2011 Taltarni, Shiraz, Victoria, South Australia *bold & robust*	38	
2012 Fritz, Pinot Noir, Russian River, California	44	11
2012 Highway 12, Cabernet Sauvignon, Sonoma, California	46	
2013 Seghesio, Zinfandel, Sonoma, South California	48	12
2012 Tikal, Amorio, Mendoza, Argentina	52	

Beers (**=on tap)

** Today's Special Brew...Ask Your Server !	6.00
** Buzzard's Bay IPA (USA)	5.50
** Cisco Grey Lady (USA)	5.50
** Guinness Stout (Ireland)	5.75
**Tuckerman's Pale Ale (USA)	5.50
Today's Special Brew...Ask Your Server !	5.50
Bass Ale (USA)	5.50
Beoks Non-Alcoholic Brew (Germany)	4.50
Budweiser or Bud Light (USA)	3.75
Coors Light (USA)	4.00
Corona Extra or Corona Light (Mexico)	5.00
Narragansett 16oz Can (USA)	3.75
Sam Adams Lager (USA)	5.50
Stella Artois (Belgium)	5.50
Yuengling Lager (USA)	3.75

From the Mixology Staff at the Bar...Margarita's & More

Slippery Mermaid... coconut vodka, blackberry puree, pineapple juice	10.00	
One Eyed Jake... with patron. grand marnier & fresh squeezed sour mix	11.00	
Eddy Traditional... with sauza hornitos tequila & triple sec	10.50	
Moscow Mule... with tito's vodka, ginger beer & lime juice	9.50	
Dark & Stormy... goslings dark rum, ginger beer & a squeeze of lime	9.50	
Sangria... traditional rojo	6.00/glass	24.00/pitcher

And Now...The Fine Print

♦ Before placing your order, please inform your server
if a person in your party has a food allergy

♦ The Back Eddy is open spring, summer & fall – ask about our hours of operation

♦ Because of the complexity of our dishes – no substitutions please !

♦ We take reservations for parties of 6 or more - on a limited basis

♦ If you bring in your own cake we charge $1.50 per person plate charge

♦ We accept Cash, Amex, Visa, Master Card, Discover & Diners – sorry, no Checks

Entrees

*Wood Grilled Yellowfin Tuna Steak... with wasabi mayo, soy & grilled fall vegetables	26.50
Wood Grilled Swordfish... with garlicky brussel sprouts, mashed potatoes & herb butter	26.50
Pan-Seared North Atlantic Salmon... with polenta, baby spinach & arudda's cream	24.50
Oven-Roasted Cod Loin... with braised white beans, kale, littlenecks & mello's chourico	25.50
1.5# Naked Sakonnet Lobster... with real butter & lemon	mkt
Fried Clams... with hand-cut fries, eddy slaw & sauce louie	mkt
Fried New Bedford Sea Scallops... with hand-cut fries eddy slaw & tartar	25.50
Classic Fish & Chips... with hand-cut fries, eddy slaw & tartar	19.50
Bacon Wrapped Giant Scallops... with macomber turnip hash & a cranberry-orange relish	29.50
Pan-Roasted Statler Chicken Breast... with white truffle oil & a hillside mushroom risotto	20.50
N.C. Style Pulled Pork Platter... with house baked beans, eddy slaw, pickles & cornbread	19.50
*Wood Grilled Brant All Natural Rib-Eye... with greens, great hill blue cheese butter & honkey fries	28.50
*Carpetbagger... rib-eye & a ½ order of fried clams	mkt

On The Side

Chicken Breast	13.50	Honkey Fries	7.00	Grilled Veg	6.00
Salmon	17.50	Hand-Cut Fries	6.00	Turnip Hash	6.00
Grilled Swordfish	19.50	Cornbread	4.00	Eddy Slaw	5.00

Kitchen Appreciation Pitcher
now you can buy the hardest working kitchen staff on the planet
a pitcher of fresh draft beer...12.00

Photos and illustrations courtesy of the Back Eddy Restaurant and the author.

Visitors

Over the past sixty plus years many well-known individuals have visited the restaurant. Some of whom have been recognized and others who have remained sub-rosa. They have not only enjoyed an adult beverage and delicious meal but they have also acquired mementos from the small retail shop, which stocks hats and T-shirts.

Many of the well-known guests become regulars when they spend time in Westport. Some own homes, others are renters, and still others are weekend guests or day-trippers from other parts of the area.

Actor Harrison Ford was a regular when he lived in town and ESPN Sportscaster Wendi Nix is a frequent customer, as was the voice of the New England Patriots for years, Gil Santos. Former CNN feature story correspondent for the show *Pinnacle*, Beverly Schuch, is also a regular.

Actor and Golden Globe Recipient, George Segal still makes an occasional appearance, as does Christopher Herren, motivational speaker and former Boston Celtic professional basketball player.

The star of the current television weekly series, *Madam Secretary*, Tea Leoni is a summer patron. Her former husband, actor David Ducovny, has also made time to come for a meal.

In the 1990s, the restaurant parking lot was always full of stickers from Langley Air Base in Washington. The owners indicated that there was a presence of CIA operatives who certainly never identified themselves as such. Norm Abrams, well known host of *This Old House* and effervescent attorney Ralph C, Martins, the first African-American DA in the history of Massachusetts (appointed by Governor William Weld), would regale their guests and staff with their stories.

Former *Boston Herald* gossip columnist and writer of the daily piece "Inside Track," Laura Raposa, and her husband, Steven Syre, former business columnist for the *Boston Globe*, spent many evenings in the restaurant. Barry Estabrook, a former contributing editor at *Gourmet Magazine*, was a frequent guest when visiting from northern New England.

Bestselling Rhode Island author Ann Hood and her husband often visit the waterfront dining facility and "love it."

Many other food critics and writers who prefer to stay under the radar are patrons, as are corporate and industry titans who visit the area on vacation.

Photo courtesy of Wikipedia.

⊙ **Ownership History**

1953-1971	"Pappy" and Evelyn Judson post Carol 1954—Sandwich Shop
1971-1974	Gratia "Topsy" Waters Moby Dick Wharf Restaurant, Inc. 1971
1974-1976	Bob and Barrie Therrien Moby Dick, Inc.
12/17/76-1985	Aime and Rita Lafrance Lafrance Wharf Restaurant, Inc.
1985-1991	Roger and Nancy Tache Moby Dick Wharf Restaurant on the Waterfront
1993 – 2006	Peter Sharp Intervivo Trust Joseph Consentino Trust The Hiftee, LLC Windward Food Service, Corp.
2007- Present	Sal Liotta and Aaron deRego River Boys, LLC

Sources

Peter Allatt
Doug Amaral
Ruth Ameil
Daniel Bogan
Captain John Borden
Julie Brown
Eben Davis
Aaron deRego
Arthur Durand
Richard Earle
Dr. Richard H. Fitton
Ann Hood
Norma Judson
David Lees
Sal Liotta
Carlton "Cukie" Macomber
Judge Joseph Macy
Everett Mills
Wendi Nix
John G. Osborne Jr.
Eleanor Rink
Kissy Russell
Beverly Schuch
Dedee Shatuck
John Sheahan
Tom and Barbara Slaight
Louise Sylvester
Dick Squire
Nancy and Roger Tache
Bernie Taradash
Barrie Throop
Karen Walsh
Olivia B. Waxman (Newsfeed Animals)
Wikipedia

Acknowledgements

Special thanks to my editor and creative specialist, historian Stefani Koorey, who masterfully coordinated this manuscript and multiple photos into this fascinating tale about a long-thriving waterfront restaurant in Westport, Massachusetts. The facility has enjoyed a great history and with many first-person interviews with owners and employees, the stories will remain in tact for future generations of locals and out of town vacationers alike.

To my long-time chum, tennis partner from childhood as well as golf opponent and still good friend, Dick Squire, who was a fisherman extraordinaire and has battled poor health for years and family tragedy with a positive attitude and spirit for all to emulate. Thank you for writing the Foreword to this book, and sharing your first-hand knowledge of the service business and the sea. Great job, Dick.

To those who have labored into the manuscript to verify the facts and write blurbs for the book—Richie Earle, Captain John Borden, and Everett Mills—your knowledge of the waterfront establishment and the sea proved invaluable to me.

To Ruth Ameil, who I have known for many years on the staff of the Acoaxet Club in Westport and someone who is always friendly and smiling but, as I found out recently about her history by accident, never divulged anything about her employment history. Thanks for adding some classic stories and photos.

About the Author

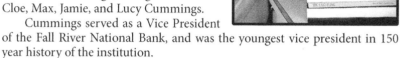

John "Red" Cummings was born in Fall River in 1945. He is the only child of Angela King and John B. Cummings, Esq. Spouse of Paula J. Francoeur, the author is the father of John B. Cummings III and David C. Cummings, and grandfather of Cloe, Max, Jamie, and Lucy Cummings.

Cummings served as a Vice President of the Fall River National Bank, and was the youngest vice president in 150 year history of the institution.

Cummings was the Chief Professional Officer of the United Way between 1978 and 1995. The funds raised in that period for the betterment of the people of Greater Fall River were double the national average .

Named Endowment and Planned Giving Director at the United Way in 1996, he was recognized for having one of the outstanding planned giving programs in the nation. He retired in 2006.

Also of Note

Cummings was elected the youngest president in the history of the Acoaxet Club in Westport, Massachusetts, and served for many years as an honorary governor.

He is a licensed real estate broker in Massachusetts and Rhode Island and is the owner of Cummings Group Realtors in Westport with his wife.

He spent years serving as volunteer assistant coach and official scorer of the Westport Middle School Girls basketball team that won 133 and lost only 12 games between 2007 and 2015.

His civic work included President of the Greater Fall River Development Corporation between 2001 to 2002, as well as chair of the Fall River Conservation Committee and Fall River Task Force on Sports and Recreation.

He is the recipient of various awards for advertising excellence and his first book, *The Last Fling, Hurricane Carol 1954, Stories from Westport, Massachusetts*, was recognized with awards from two national book festivals. He was also the producer of a documentary film by the same name and coauthored a book, *From Little Acorns to Giant Oaks*, about the history of the Greater Fall River Development Corporation and the economic development in Fall River. His most recent writing is *Cream of the Crop Fall River's Best and Brightest*. It is a collection of 260 mini biographies of those educated in the Spindle City who became highly successful as well as includes a list of public figures, undefeated and state championship sports teams, and military heroes who died in various wars. The book is being taught as part of the B.M.C. Durfee High School curriculum and over twenty individuals featured in the book have appeared in class to speak with the students.

$13.95

In Praise of
Lobstah Tales

John 'Red' Cummings is the recipient of various awards for advertising excellence. His first book, *The Last Fling, Hurricane Carol 1954, Stories from Westport, Massachusetts*, was recognized with awards from two national book festivals. His most recent writing is *Cream of the Crop: Fall River's Best and Brightest*. It is a collection of 260 mini biographies of those educated in the Spindle City who became highly successful.

Hillside Media
46 Hillside Road
Westport, MA 02790
HillsideMedia.net